Learn About Urban Life

Life in an Industrial City

Lizann Flatt

Crabtree Publishing Company

www.crabtreebooks.com

Author: Lizann Flatt
Editor-in-Chief: Lionel Bender
Editors: Simon Adams and Molly Aloian
Proofreader: Adrianna Morganelli
Project coordinator: Kathy Middleton
Photo research: Ben White
Designer and makeup: Ben White
Production coordinator: Amy Salter
Production: Kim Richardson
Prepress technician: Amy Salter
Consultant: Amy Caldera, M.Sc., Elementary School Publishing Consultant, Writer, and Former Teacher

Main cover photo: A refinery stands in the background as a barge delivering goods moves along the Houston ship channel
Inset cover photo: Washing the car is family time.

This book was produced for Crabtree Publishing Company by Bender Richardson White.

Photographs and reproductions:
© Bigstockphoto.com: page 29 (Arteki)
© Blend Images/Fotosearch: cover inset
© Getty Images: pages 5 (Michael Matisse), 10 (EightFish), 16 (Skip Brown), 21 (George Doyle), 22 (ThinkStock), 25 (Mark Wilson)
© Greater Houston Convention and Visitors Bureau: pages 12, 13, 15, 19, 20, 24, 26
© iStockphoto.com: cover main image (John Zellmer), pages 27 (Globestock), 28 (Jonathan Larsen)
© www.shutterstock.com: Headline image and pages 1 (Winthrop Brookhouse), 4 (Howard Sandler), 6 (Jeremy Richards), 7 (Gary Blakeley), 9 (SV Lumagraphica), 11 (Gregory James Van Raalte), 17 (Christian Langerek)
© Topfoto: pages 8 (The Image Works), 14 (Curt Tech Postcard Archive/HIP), 18 (Lightroom Photos/NASA), 23 (The Image Works)

Acknowledgments:
Special thanks to Mary Wade, resident of Houston, for providing and verifying information about her city.

Library and Archives Canada Cataloguing in Publication

Flatt, Lizann
       Life in an industrial city / Lizann Flatt.

(Learn about urban life)
Includes index.
ISBN 978-0-7787-7392-4 (bound).--ISBN 978-0-7787-7402-0 (pbk.)

       1. City and town life--Juvenile literature. 2. Industrial sites--Juvenile literature. 3. Company towns--Juvenile literature. 4. Houston (Tex.)--Juvenile literature. I. Title. II. Series: Learn about urban life

HT152.F53 2010   j307.76'6   C2009-906248-8

Library of Congress Cataloging-in-Publication Data

Flatt, Lizann.
   Life in an industrial city / Lizann Flatt.
       p. cm. -- (Learn about urban life)
   Includes index.
   ISBN 978-0-7787-7402-0 (pbk. : alk. paper) --
   ISBN 978-0-7787-7392-4 (reinforced library binding : alk. paper)
  1. City and town life--Juvenile literature. 2. City and town life--Texas--Houston--Juvenile literature. 3. Company towns--Juvenile literature. 4. Houston (Tex.)--Juvenile literature. I. Title. II. Series.

HT152.F58 2010
307.76--dc22

2009042422

Crabtree Publishing Company
www.crabtreebooks.com   1-800-387-7650

Printed in the USA/122009/BG20091103

Copyright © 2010 CRABTREE PUBLISHING COMPANY. All rights reserved. No part of this publication may be reproduced, stored in a retrieval system or be transmitted in any form or by any means, electronic, mechanical, photocopying, recording, or otherwise, without the prior written permission of Crabtree Publishing Company. In Canada: We acknowledge the financial support of the Government of Canada through the Book Publishing Industry Development Program (BPIDP) for our publishing activities.

Published in Canada
Crabtree Publishing
616 Welland Ave.
St. Catharines, Ontario
L2M 5V6

Published in the United States
Crabtree Publishing
PMB 59051
350 Fifth Avenue, 59th Floor
New York, New York 10118

Published in the United Kingdom
Crabtree Publishing
Maritime House
Basin Road North, Hove
BN41 1WR

Published in Australia
Crabtree Publishing
386 Mt. Alexander Rd.
Ascot Vale (Melbourne)
VIC 3032

Contents

Urban Areas	4
Everyday Needs	6
Being Big	8
Districts and Zones	10
Welcome to Houston	12
The Industrial Area	14
A City At Work	16
The Working Day	18
On the Move	20
Home Life	22
Under Control	24
Changing Lifestyle	26
Industry Around the World	28
Facts and Figures	30
Glossary	31
Further Information and Index	32

Urban Areas

Cities and towns are places where thousands of people live and work close together. These places are called **urban areas**. Places with far fewer people, such as towns, are called **rural areas**. Most urban areas are filled with schools, houses, stores, office buildings, and parks. Roads are busy with **pedestrians** and traffic.

▼ The city of Ottawa, Canada, is an urban area. A lot of buildings close together line the Ottawa River.

▲ City streets can be narrow and sometimes crowded with people, like this street in Paris, France.

Within a city, there are many **neighborhoods**. A neighborhood is an area where many people live, shop, and play together. Most cities have a central "downtown" area, with many offices and stores, and areas near a seaport or railroad for **factories**. These areas for factories are known as **industrial** areas. This book will focus on Houston, Texas, a city in the United States with a lot of industry.

Everyday Needs

Whether people live in urban or rural areas, they need food, clean water, and shelter. They also need **energy** such as electricity to light and heat their homes and to cook their food. These essential items are called **resources**. In a city, large amounts of resources must be delivered to large numbers of people every day.

▲ At a market in the city of Kolkata, India, people can buy fish and other fresh foods brought in from rural areas.

▲ In a city, many families live near each other. Large areas for houses—known as residential areas—are often located at the edge of a city.

Cities are often located on a sea coast, or on the shore of a large river or lake. There, the people of the city use the water for drinking, cleaning, and as a **transportation** route. Other natural resources such as oil or food from farms are brought in from the surrounding areas. Factories, stores, schools, and offices in the city provide jobs for a lot of workers.

Being Big

A city must provide resources and **services** for its many thousands of **residents**. A city needs housing areas, a transportation system to move people around the city quickly, and lights that illuminate the city streets. Cities need to deliver water to millions of homes and businesses, and need underground sewers to take away wastewater and rainwater.

▼ City stores are often huge so many people can shop at once. The stores can become crowded.

Big cities face problems with having a lot of people. Roads can become so crowded with cars and trucks that traffic jams happen. Cities have to collect and safely dispose of tons of trash. Cities can run out of land to put houses on or places to put garbage. **Pollution** or smog made by **exhaust** from cars, factories, and buildings can make the air unhealthy to breathe.

▲ Cities need to have sidewalks so that people have a safe route away from traffic to walk where they need to go.

Districts and Zones

Cities often make rules or **laws** about the types of buildings and activities allowed in the different areas of the city. These areas are called districts or zones. Factories operate in industrial districts. **Commercial** districts are for businesses, such as offices and stores. Residential districts are areas where people live.

▼ Factories are usually located far from residential zones. These power plants in the industrial zone of Johor, Malaysia, spew steam into the sky.

Districts or zones make sure homes are not built near the worst noise and pollution from factories or the busy traffic from commercial districts. Near houses and offices, areas can be set aside for parks where people can relax and play. But zones can also mean people have to travel far from their homes to shop in the commercial zones. Or they may have to **commute** for long distances to work in industrial districts.

▶ City parks, such as Central Park in New York City, give residents places to relax. Some cities also have laws regulating the size of buildings, such as skyscrapers.

Welcome to Houston

Houston is a big city in Texas. It takes up an area of 634 square miles (1,642 sq km). With a **population** of 2,140,000, it is the fourth largest city in the United States. Houstonians, people who live in Houston, come from many different backgrounds, including European, Hispanic, African, Middle Eastern, and Asian.

▼ Houston is called the energy capital of the world. More than 5,000 energy-related companies have offices here.

▲ A map of North America showing Houston in the state of Texas. Houston is located near the Gulf of Mexico on the Atlantic Ocean.

Downtown Houston is full of tall office towers, restaurants, three sports stadiums, and a theater district. Underground walkways for pedestrians connect office buildings. The Buffalo Bayou waterway winds through the downtown area. Other neighborhoods in the city include the Museum District, the Theater District, Midtown, the Galleria, the Medical Center, and Chinatown. Houston also has many industrial areas.

▲ Midtown is a pleasant neighborhood in Houston with high-rise living spaces, art galleries, and wide sidewalks for pedestrians to use.

The Industrial Area

Houston was founded in 1836, when two brothers bought land on Buffalo Bayou to start a city. They named the spot Houston and advertised for people to live there. In the 1850s, Houston became an important port and railroad center. Early industry was built around cotton and lumber. In the early 1900s, the city improved its harbor, and oil was discovered nearby.

▼ This view of Main Street, Houston, dates from 1940. It shows brick buildings. Today's Main Street buildings are made of glass and steel, and they are much, much taller.

Houston has no clearly marked industrial zones because its residents voted against making any zone laws. But there are rules about how land is used. For example, there are rules stating the minimum sizes for housing lots. Despite the lack of zones, many factories or plants are found along the Houston ship channel. Here, factories have easy access to the transportation systems that deliver the materials they need to make things.

▲ The Port of Houston is the tenth largest in the world. Many factories and oil storage and processing plants are located along the 25-mile (40-km) ship channel.

A City At Work

In a normal working day, ships enter and exit the Port of Houston. They are guided to dock by tugboats. Cranes unload or load ship **cargo** such as containers of consumer goods, grain, petroleum, iron, or steel. Trucks or trains take away the cargo to be sold. Some cargo goes to **warehouses** in the city, where it is stored until sold.

▲ In Houston harbor, factory goods are loaded into vast container ships. The cargo is then taken and sold to other parts of the world.

Factories and warehouses use lots of energy for heating in cool weather and air conditioning in hot weather. Workers need lighting to do their jobs. Machines operate on electricity. The electricity is delivered to Houston through electrical wires that stretch to power-generating plants all over Texas. Some workplaces such as hospitals have their own electricity generators. If the power goes out, they can still operate.

▼ Oil factory or plant workers like this engineer check machinery and pipes to make sure all the machinery is in good working order.

The Working Day

Many factories in Houston operate 24 hours a day because there is so much work to be done. But people cannot work all day. They need time off to relax, sleep, or be with their families. So workdays are organized in time periods called shifts. While one shift of people works, another shift sleeps.

▼ Workers at the Houston Space Center work in shifts to keep a constant eye on the systems that help astronauts in space.

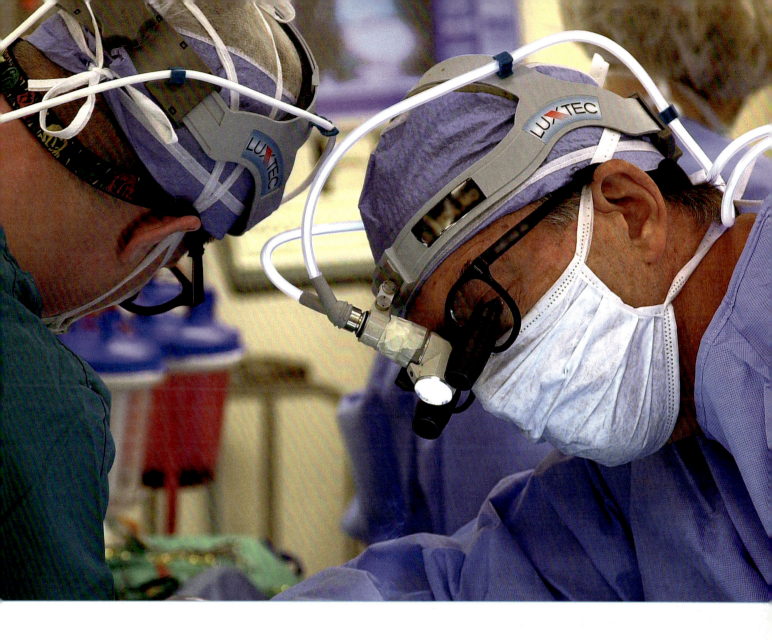

▲ Doctors, nurses, and many other hospital workers all work shifts. They are needed to do their jobs at all hours of the day or night.

Shiftworkers may work from 7:00 a.m. to 3:00 p.m., or 3:00 p.m. to 11:00 p.m., or 11:00 p.m. to 7:00 a.m. They may work for any five days of a week and then have two days off. Most office workers do not work shifts. They work from 9:00 a.m. to 5:00 p.m. Monday to Friday. All workers have a break for lunch in the middle of the workday.

On the Move

Most Houstonians commute to work by car. Highways are busy from 5:30 a.m. to 9:00 a.m. when many people arrive at work, and again from 3:30 p.m. to 7:00 p.m. when they go home. People who work downtown can take buses, taxis, or the light rail system, called MetroRail. It is a railroad of fast and quiet trains made to move people from place to place.

▼ The Metro, or Houston light rail system, moves people quickly between certain neighborhoods and downtown.

Trucks use highways to move goods between factories and warehouses within Houston. A network of roads, railroad lines, and two major airports are used to move products to the rest of the continent and the world. Ships are loaded up with cargo to sell at the Port of Houston and sail to other parts of the world including Mexico, Brazil, Belgium, the Netherlands, and Venezuela.

▶ Highways fill with traffic taking people and goods in and out of Houston.

Home Life

Many residents live in **suburban** areas on the north, west, and south sides of the city. People shop at large indoor malls and strip malls. One mall, the Galleria, even has a skating rink in its center for families to enjoy. Houston Parks and Recreation Department runs 350 parks and some 200 green spaces including golf courses, dog parks, skate parks, pools, and hiking and biking trails.

▼ Houston families and friends often spend their leisure time visiting the city's **local** attractions, such as the aquarium.

◀ These Houston high school students are fixing a traffic camera for a school technology project.

Houston has almost 300 public schools and many **private schools**. It has many colleges and several medical schools. At the 57 **community** centers, residents can take courses or participate in recreational sports. There are public libraries downtown with neighborhood branches all over the city. Houston also has a large zoo, aquarium, and a children's museum.

Under Control

Hurricanes and tropical storms threaten Houston every year. Emergencies can happen at any time. Houston industries are prepared. In case of fires or the release of **toxic** fumes, refineries and chemical plants have their own firefighting crews. Each worker has a job to do in an emergency and knows the company safety plans.

▼ In emergencies or after accidents, Houston's air ambulance flies people to city hospitals. The ambulance flies at any time of the day, 365 days of the year.

Many factories have security guards to look after their buildings. Security at the Port of Houston uses cameras, patrol boats and cars, and all-terrain vehicles to keep the area and its workers safe. The city has its own firefighters and police officers. Hospitals, doctors, and nurses are always ready to help people in emergencies.

▼ Heavy rains during hurricanes or tropical storms can mean flooding in Houston streets.

Changing Lifestyle

Houston has long been working to attract different industries to the city. The city already has chemical plants, oil refineries, and shipping and manufacturing companies. Companies researching space, science, medicine, communication technology, and new energy sources such as solar power are now moving here.

▼ The Children's Museum was started by parents who wanted to help educate all kids in Houston. The museum entertains and educates children in English and Spanish.

The Port of Houston has allowed some of its land and waterways to be used to breed oysters and for birds to make their homes. To cut down on traffic jams, specific lanes on highways can only be used by vehicles with several passengers. To reduce air pollution, city services are using **hybrid vehicles**. Houston also allows residents to use areas of some city parks to grow their own food.

▶ Wind turbines are a newer, cleaner form of energy technology. Houston is buying electricity made by these turbines in other parts of Texas for the city to use.

Industry Around the World

Around the world, many cities rely on factories and industries to make money and create jobs. These cities all have transportation routes to get materials to their factories and to get finished products out to the world. For example, Detroit, U.S.A.; Yokohama, Japan; Shanghai, China; and Mumbai, India, are all cities with a lot of industry.

▲ Shanghai, China, has one of the busiest ports in the world for container ships.

▲ Inside a factory where cars are made. Automobile manufacturing is a large and important industry in North America, Japan, and other parts of Asia.

Many industries follow their country's laws to be sure their workers are healthy and safe at work, and have enough pay. The industries also take care not to harm the environment. In other parts of the world, there are few industrial laws. In those cities some workers are overworked, underpaid, and factories make a lot of pollution.

Facts and Figures

General's name
Houston is named after General Sam Houston. He was president of the Republic of Texas before Texas joined the United States of America in 1845.

NASA
Houston is famous for NASA, the National Aeronautics and Space Administration. Its Lyndon B. Johnson Space Center monitors all U.S. space flights.

Hungry Houston
There are more than 11,000 restaurants in Houston. The city claims more Houstonians eat out than residents of any other city.

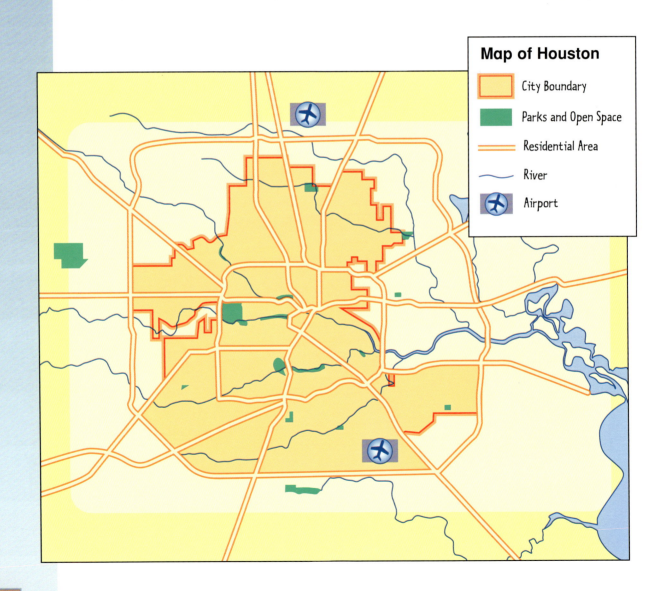

Map of Houston
- City Boundary
- Parks and Open Space
- Residential Area
- River
- Airport

Glossary

cargo Goods or products carried by a vehicle

city Large urban area, with thousands or millions of people and many houses, offices, roads, and factories

commercial To do with buying and selling of goods and services

community A group of people who live together, share their environment, and help each other

commute To travel long distances between home and work every day

energy The power to do work. It can come from burning fuels such as coal or oil, or from wind, water, and the Sun

exhaust Gases given off by an engine

factories Businesses where machines are used to make something so it can then be sold. Also called a plant

hurricane A violent tropical storm

hybrid vehicles Cars that run on two forms of power, usually gas and electricity

industrial To do with trading or making goods for sale

law A rule made by the government of the country or city that must be obeyed by everyone living there

local People or places that are nearby

neighborhood An area where people live, work, and relax together

pedestrians People who are walking, usually on a sidewalk or roadside

pollution Dirt or unclean substances carried in the air or water

population The total number of people who live in an area

private school A school started and operated without using any government or other public money

residents People who live in a place such as a city, a country, or in a house or apartment

resources Things one needs or must have

rural areas Small, quiet places to live in the countryside

services Things all living areas need, such as street lighting and cleaning, healthcare, policing, firefighting, and garbage collection

suburban Mostly residential areas outside the city center

toxic A substance that is poisonous

transportation Moving things from one place to another, or a subway or bus system that does this

urban areas Built-up places such as a city or large town

warehouse A large building where goods are stored until moved somewhere else

Further Information

FURTHER READING
Book of Cities. Piero Ventura, Universe Publishing, 2009
City Lullaby. Marilyn Singer, Clarion Books, 2007
City Signs. Zoran Milich, Kids Can Press, 2005
Sam Houston: Standing Firm. Mary Dodson Wade, Bright Sky Press, 2009
What is a Community: From A to Z. Bobbie Kalman, Crabtree Publishers, 2000
Wow! City! Robert Neubecker, Hyperion Children's Books, 2004

WEB SITES
Houston History: http://www.houstonhistory.com/
The Houston Zoo: http://www.houstonzoo.org/
Children's Museum of Houston: http://www.cmhouston.org/
For Kids Only, Earth Science from NASA: http://kids.earth.nasa.gov/
Smog City-air pollution: http://www.smogcity.com
Texas Railroad Commission's Kids Page: http://kids.rrc.state.tx.us/

Index

air ambulance 24
cargo 16
Central Park, New York 11
cities 4, 5, 6, 7, 8, 9, 10
city services 8
commercial districts 10, 11
commuting 11, 20
districts or zones 10, 11
energy 6, 17, 27
factories 5, 10, 17, 18, 25, 28, 29
firefighters 24, 25
hospitals 17, 19, 25
Houston 12, 13, 15, 17, 21, 23, 26, 30
Houston, Downtown 13
Houston harbor 14, 16
Houston, history of 14, 30
Houston, Midtown 13

Houston, population 12
Houston ship channel 15
Houston Space Center 18, 30
hurricanes 24, 25
industrial districts 5, 10, 15
industry 26, 28, 29
Johor, Malaysia 10
Kolkata, India 6
laws 10, 11
leisure 22, 23
libraries 23
Main Street 14
NASA 30
neighborhoods 5
Ottawa, Canada 4
Paris, France 5
parks 11, 22
pedestrians 4

police officers 25
pollution 9, 11, 27, 29
Port of Houston 15, 16, 21, 25, 27
residential districts 7, 10
residents 8
resources 6, 7
restaurants 30
rural areas 4
schools and colleges 7, 23
Shanghai, China 29
shiftwork 18, 19
sidewalks 9
stores 8
street markets 6
suburbs 7, 22
transportation 7, 15, 20, 21
urban areas 4
zones 10, 11, 15